Ludwig van Beethoven
(1770-1827)

Rondi
Kleine Sonaten
Sonatinen

für Klavier · for piano · pour piano

Urtext

INDEX

Rondo in C

WoO 48
1783

Rondo in A

Rondo in C

Op. 51, No. 1
1796-97

à Mlle la Comtesse Henriette de Lichnowsky

Rondo in G

Op. 51, No. 2
1800

Andante cantabile e grazioso

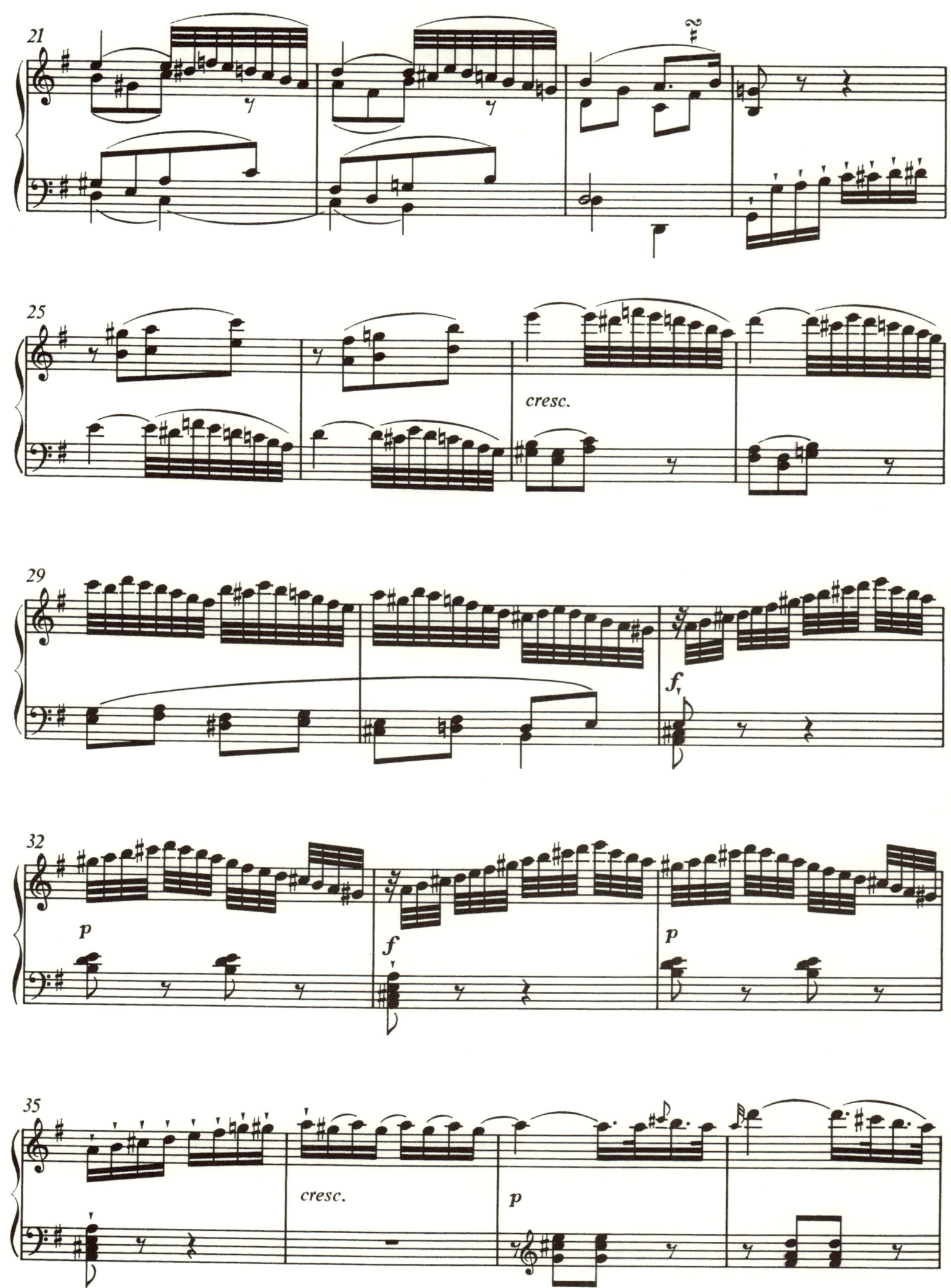

K 198

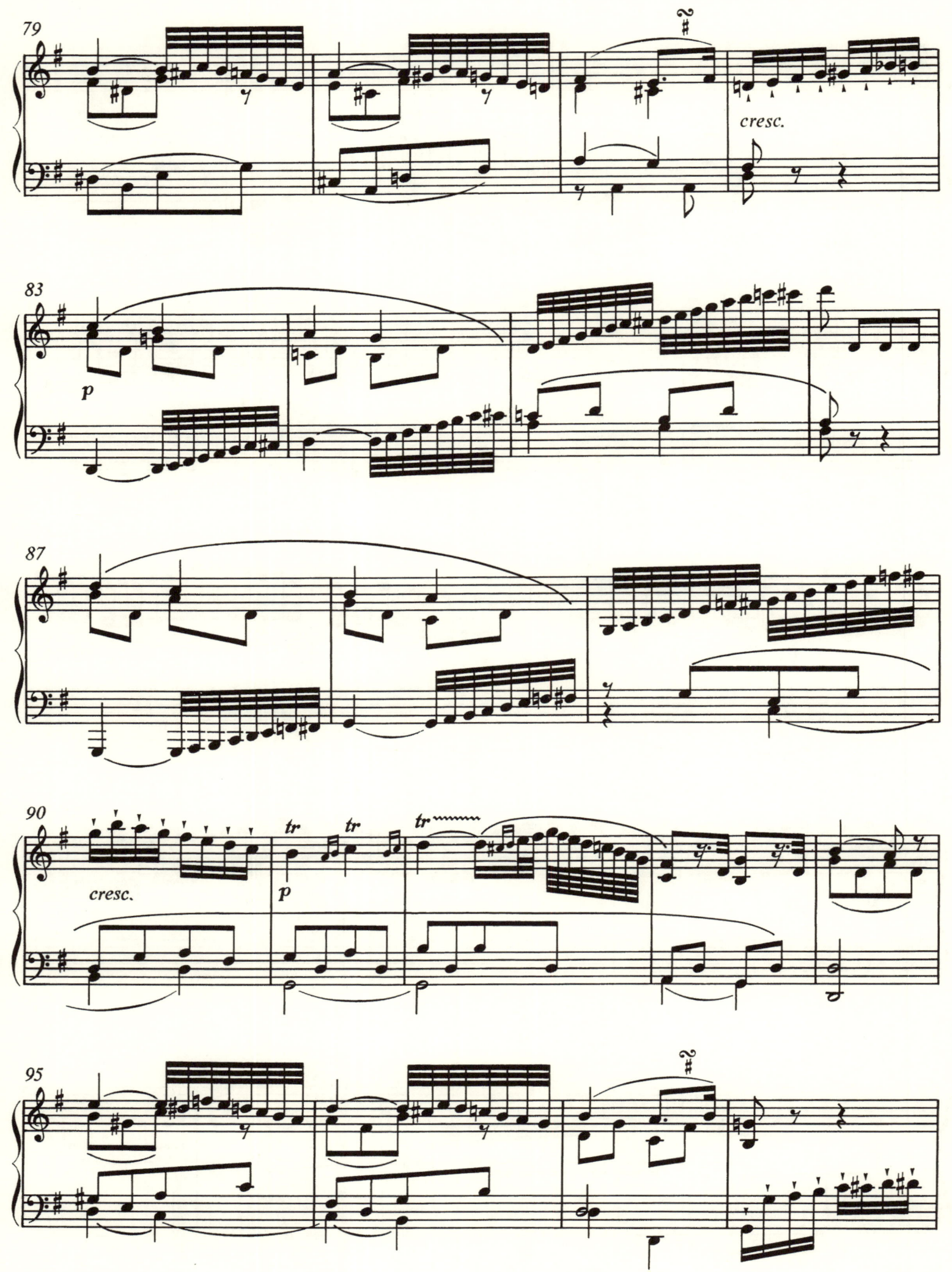

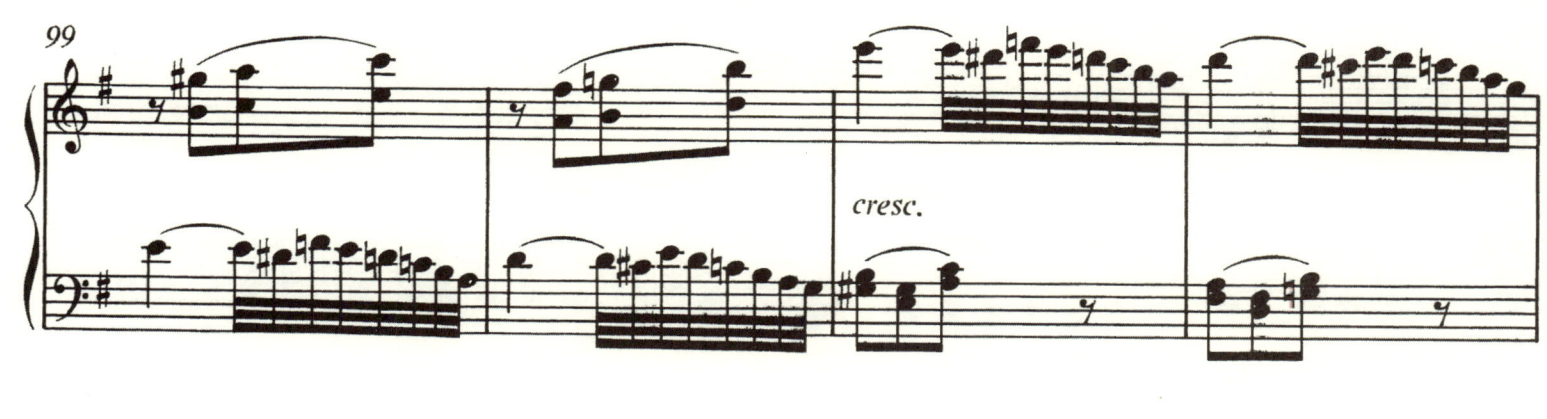

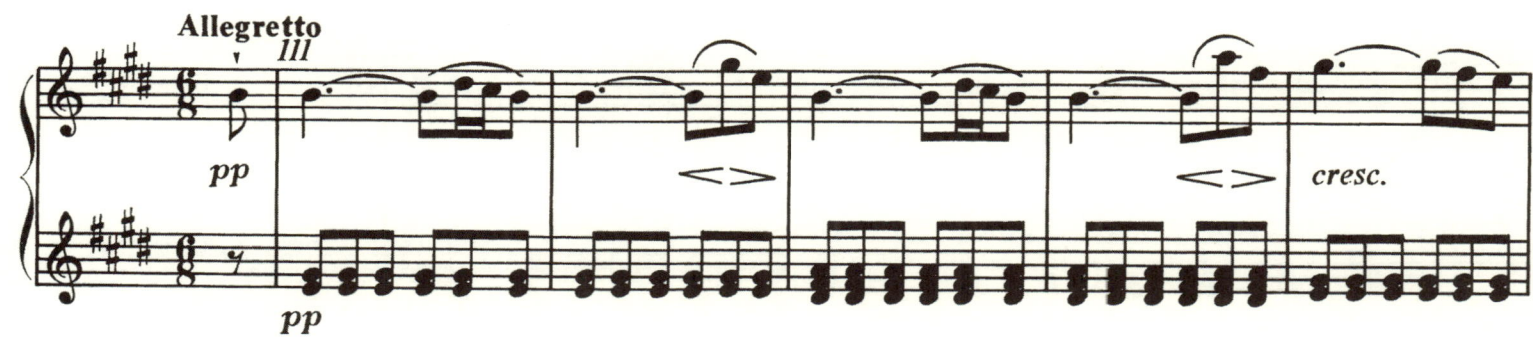

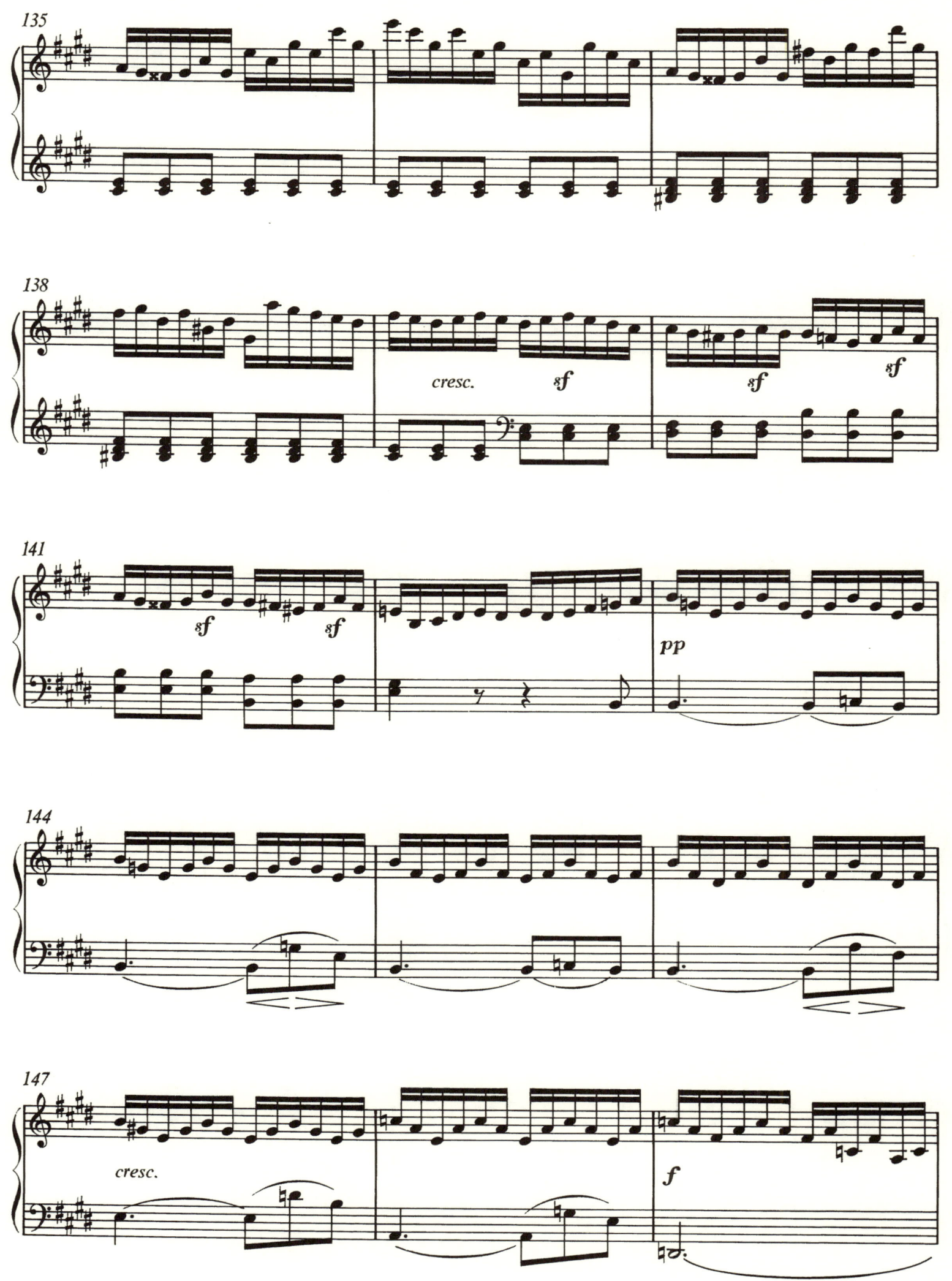

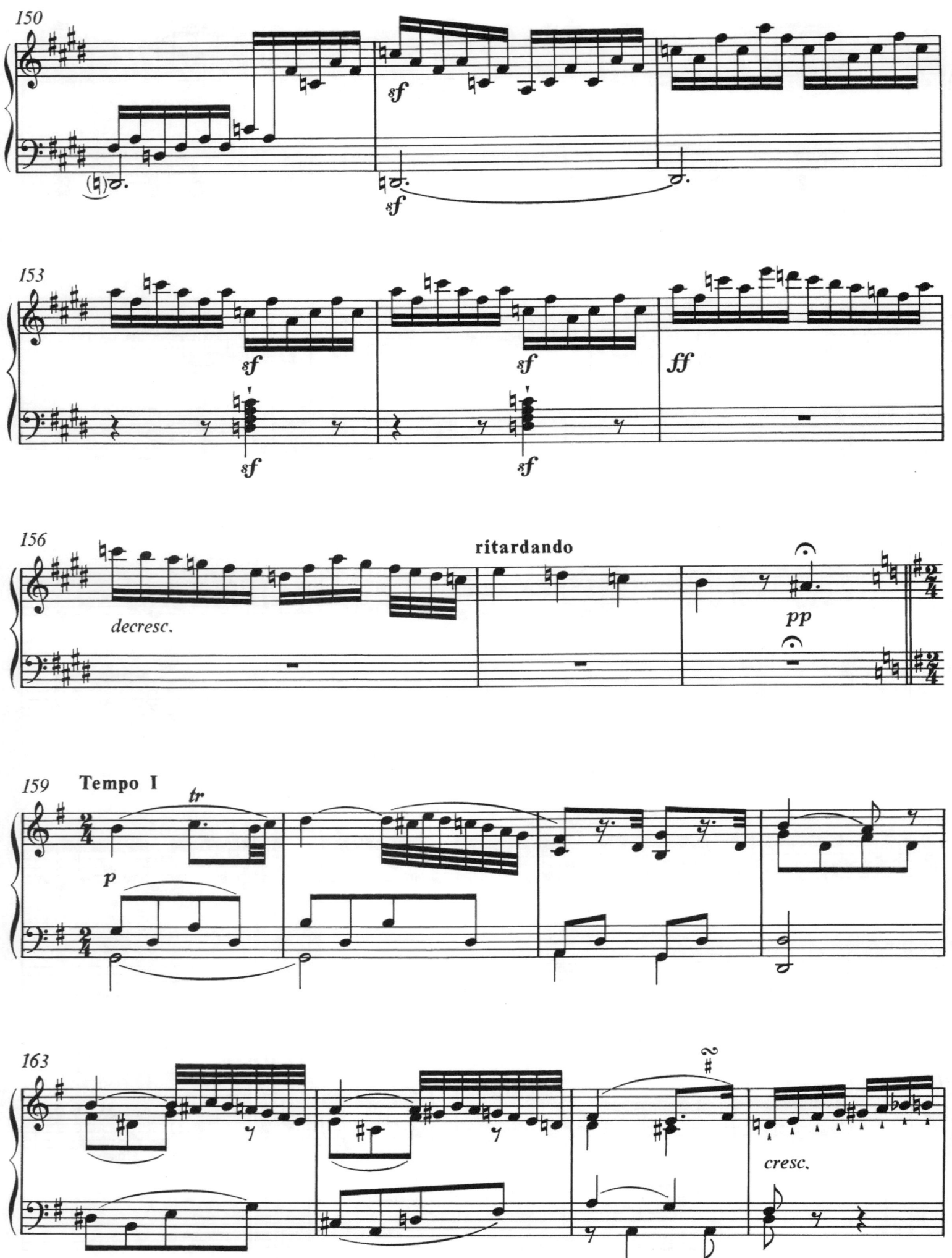

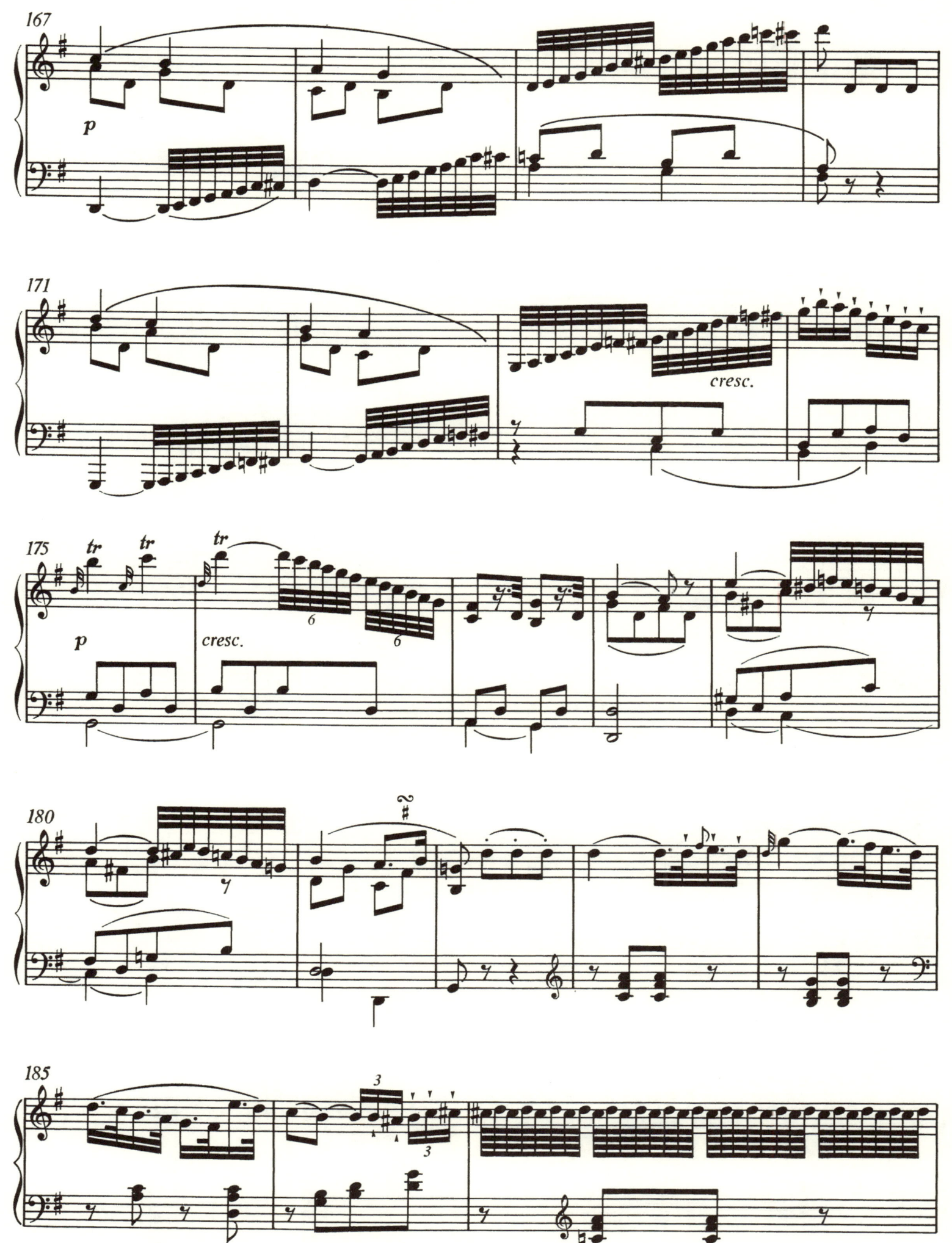

Leichte Kaprice
(Rondo a capriccio)

Dem Erzbischofe und Kurfürsten zu Köln, Maximilian Friedrich gewidmet

3 Sonaten

Sonate in Es

WoO 47/1
1782-83

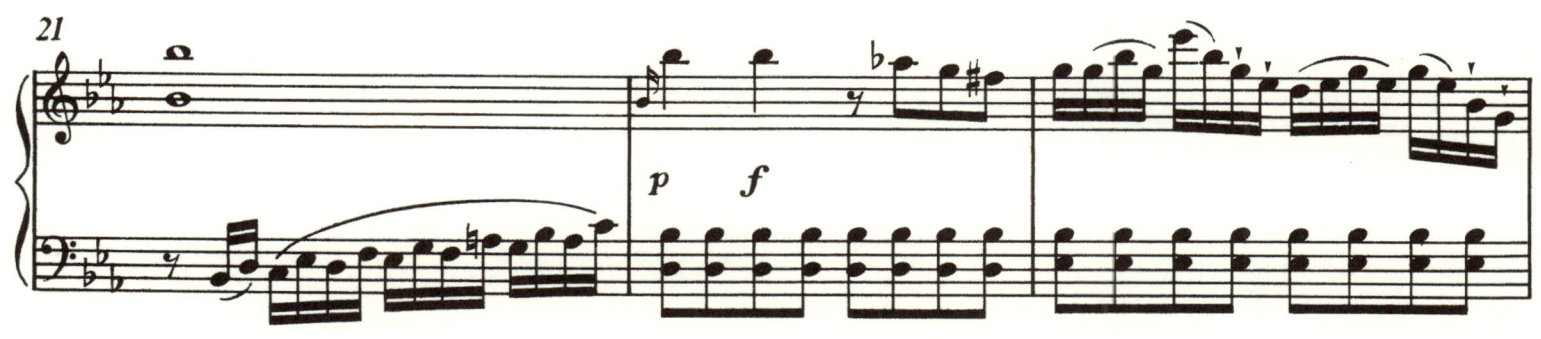

Sonate in f

WoO 47/2
1782-83

Larghetto maestoso

Allegro assai

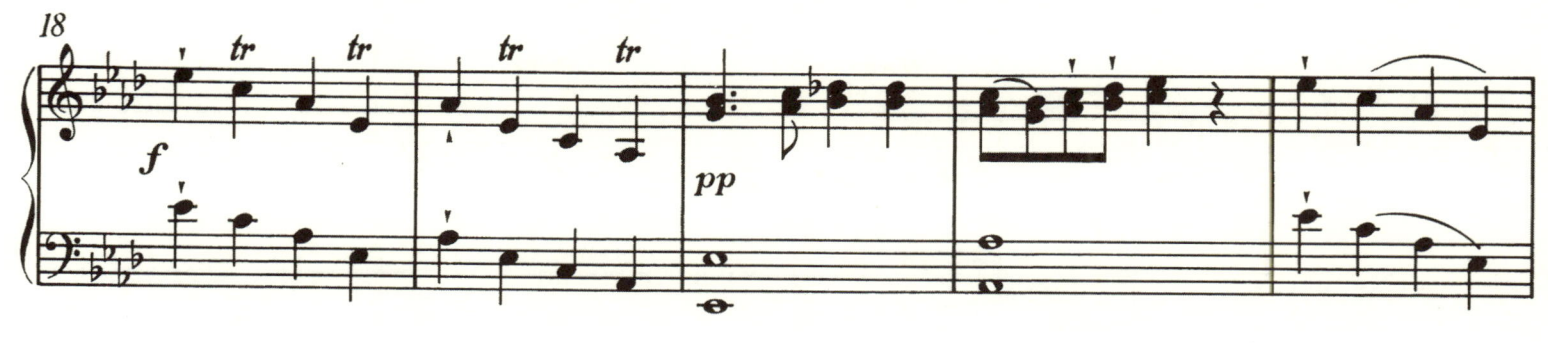

K 198

Sonate in D

WoO 47/3
1782-83

Allegro

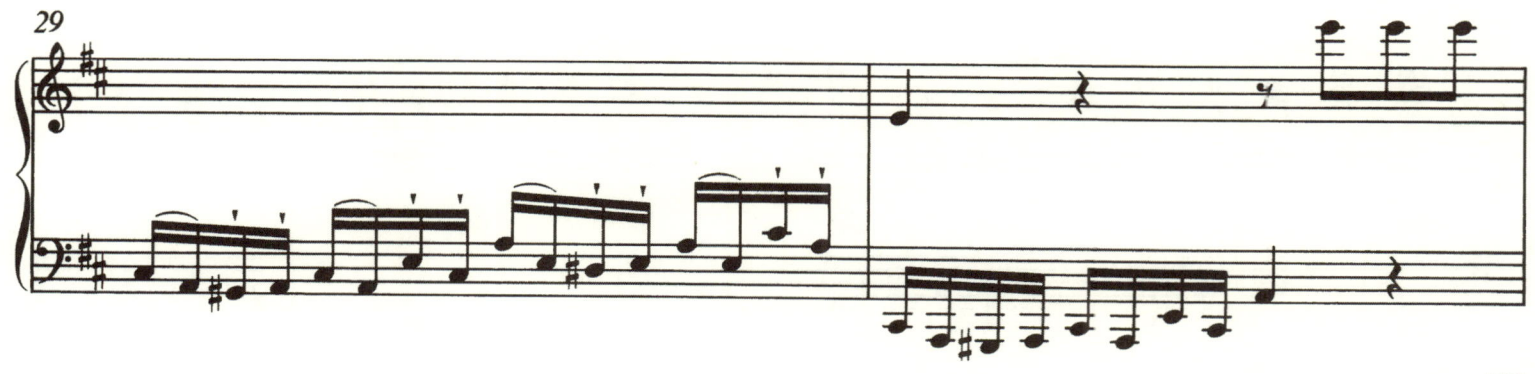

Scherzando
Allegro, ma non troppo

Für F.G. Wegeler geschrieben

[Sonatine in F]

WoO 50
1788-90

Allegretto

à Mlle Eleonore de Breuning

[Sonate in C]

WoO 51
1791-92

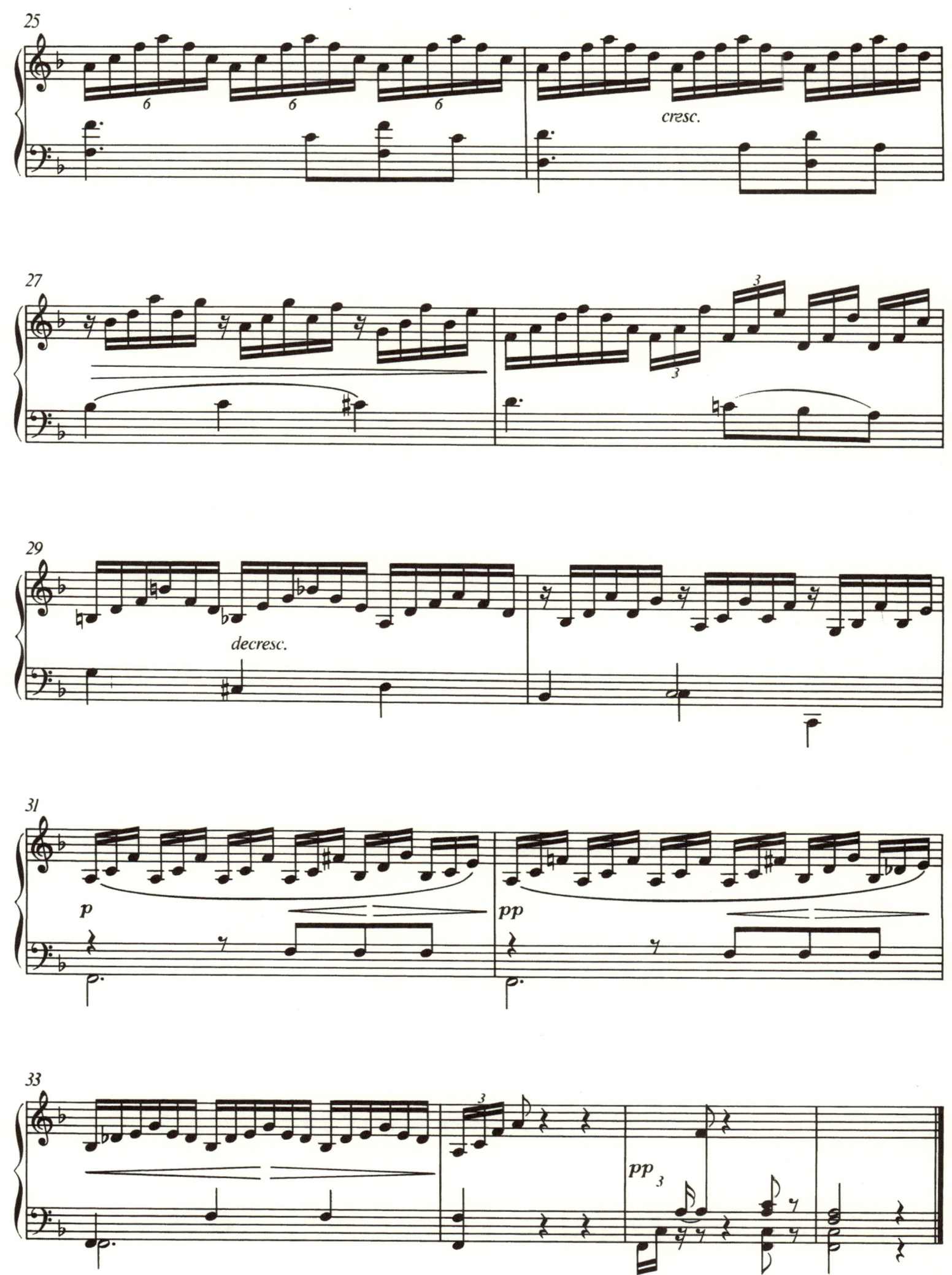

2 Sonatinen

Kinsky-Halm Anh. 5

1.

Romanze

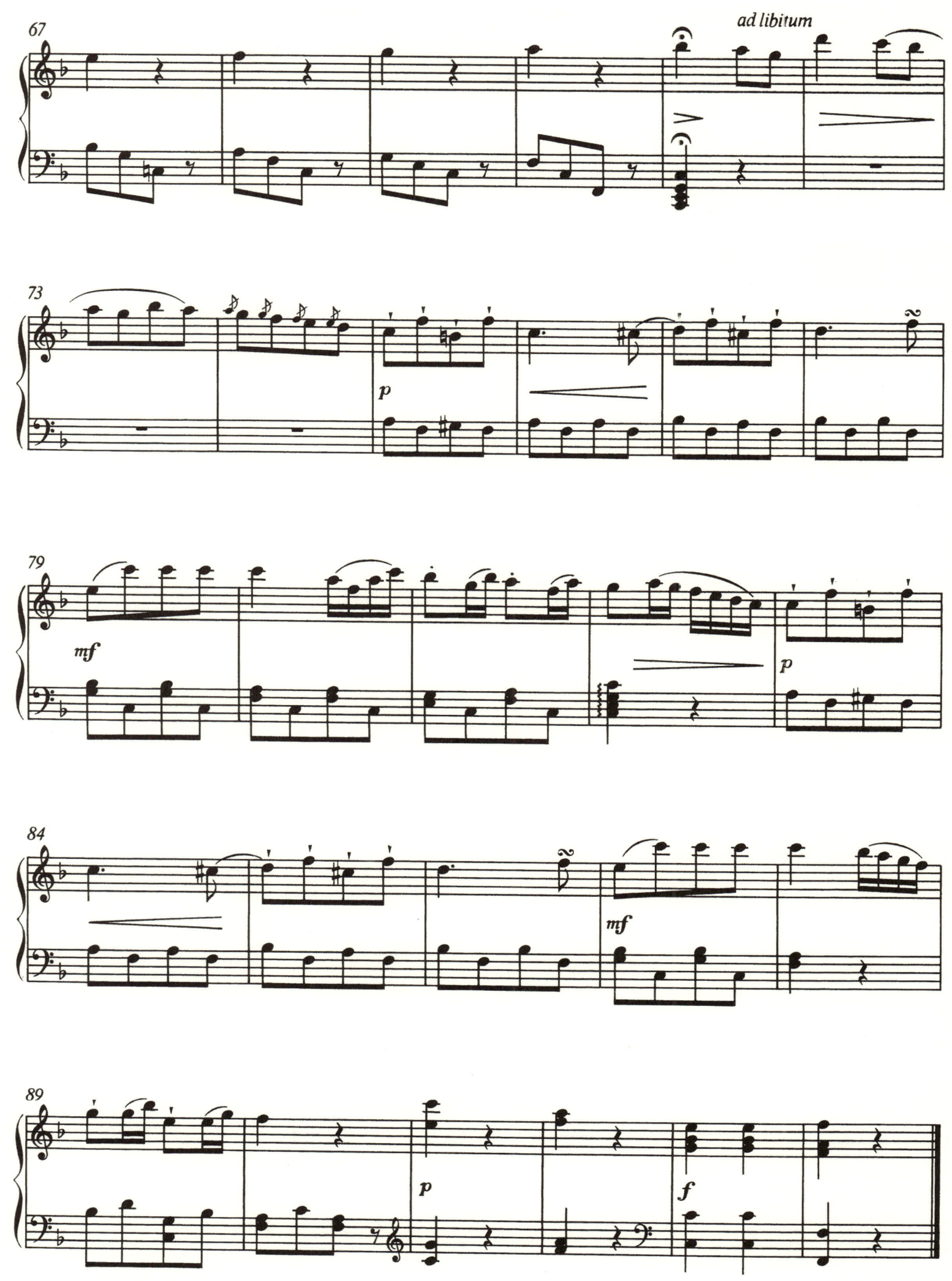

MUSICA PIANO

OVER 25.000 PAGES OF PIANO MUSIC SHEETS ONLINE

Bach, Beethoven, Brahms, Chopin, Czerny, Debussy, Gershwin, Dvořák, Grieg, Haydn, Joplin, Lyadov, Mendelssohn-Bartholdy, Mozart, Mussorgsky, Purcell, Schubert, Schumann, Scriabin, Tchaikovsky and many more

KÖNEMANN

© 2018 koenemann.com GmbH
www.koenemann.com

Editor: István Máriássy
Responsible co-editor: Tamás Záskaliczky
Technical editor: Desző Varga
Engraved by Kottamester Bt., Budapest

critical notes available on www.frechmann.com

ISBN 978-3-7419-1422-5

Printed in China by Reliance Printing

K 198